WITHDR

P9-DYP-475

The Comanche

KEVIN CUNNINGHAM
AND PETER BENOIT

Children's Press®
An Imprint of Scholastic Inc.
New York Toronto London Auckland Sydney
Mexico City New Delhi Hong Kong
Danbury, Connecticut

Content Consultant
Scott Manning Stevens, PhD
Director, McNickle Center
Newberry Library
Chicago, Illinois

Library of Congress Cataloging-in-Publication Data

Cunningham, Kevin, 1966–
  The Comanche/Kevin Cunningham and Peter Benoit.
      p. cm.—(A true book)
  Includes bibliographical references and index.
  ISBN-13: 978-0-531-20770-3 (lib. bdg.)   978-0-531-29312-6 (pbk.)
  ISBN-10: 0-531-20770-6 (lib. bdg.)   0-531-29312-2 (pbk.)
  1. Comanche Indians—Juvenile literature. I. Benoit, Peter, 1955– II. Title.
  E99.C85C86 2011
  978.004'974572—dc22   2010049081

All rights reserved. Published in 2011 by Children's Press, an imprint of Scholastic Inc.
Printed in China 62
SCHOLASTIC, CHILDREN'S PRESS, A TRUE BOOK and associated logos are trademarks and/or registered trademarks of Scholastic Inc.

1 2 3 4 5 6 7 8 9 10 R 19 18 17 16 15 14 13 12 11

Find the Truth!

Everything you are about to read is true *except* for one of the sentences on this page.

Which one is **TRUE**?

T or F   Comanches played a vital role in World War II.

T or F   The outer covering of Comanche teepees was made of heavyweight cotton.

Find the answers in this book.

Contents

THE BIG TRUTH!

**Comanche hunters
on a buffalo hunt**

Baby in a cradleboard

Many Comanche men plucked their eyebrows and facial hair.

This map shows where the Comanche lived before the 1800s, where they migrated in the mid-1800s, and where their **reservation** is today.

Hudson Bay

Canada

Pacific Ocean

Wyoming

Nebraska

United States

Colorado

Kansas

Atlantic Ocean

New Mexico

Oklahoma

Texas

N
W   E
S

Gulf of Mexico

Mexico

LEGEND

Comanche lands before 1800s

Comanche migration

Comanche lands mid-1800s

Present-day Comanche Reservation

Traders, Raiders, and Warriors

The Comanche first appeared as a group in the 1600s. Before that, they were part of the Shoshone people of Wyoming and lived along the Upper Platte River. The Comanche separated from the Shoshone as they moved away to look for horses. Before 1492, there were no horses in North America. Then, Spanish explorers and settlers introduced them. Native American peoples, especially the Comanche, soon took to the useful animals.

The name *Comanche* comes from a Ute word meaning "enemies."

A Comanche travels on horseback. In many Comanche groups, there were more horses than people.

On the Move

Riding on horseback made the Comanche more **mobile**, and they began to look for better hunting grounds. First, the Comanche followed bison (buffalo) herds deeper into the Great Plains. Other Shoshone soon joined them. In time, the Comanche dominated a huge area of the Plains and central Texas called the Comancheria (koh-MAN-cher-ee-ah). Their attention soon turned from hunting bison to keeping horses. In the 1800s, Comanche traders sold horses to American settlers, Spanish traders, and other Plains peoples.

Raiding

The Comanche roamed a huge area that contained more than 2 million wild horses. They captured and tamed some of them for sale. But Comanche riders also stole farm animals from other Plains peoples, as well as from American and Mexican settlers. Though raiding led to bad feelings and even war, Comanche **tradition** considered it acceptable and manly to raid others for profit.

Capturing wild horses was a way for young Comanche men to show their skill and bravery.

Controlling a wild horse could be dangerous work.

Travelers passing through Comanche land scared off many bison. The Comanche sometimes raided wagon trains for food.

Raids took place at night under a full moon that settlers on the Plains and in northern Mexico called the Comanche moon. These raids were common throughout the 1800s. Comanche raiders took more than horses, however. Food was important, as were weapons and cattle. The Comanche also took women and older children as captives and slaves. Men were killed.

Life as a Captive

The Comanche kept white captives for many reasons. Some they sold back to their families for guns or other items. Others were made slaves. Most were mistreated. A few, however, became members of the band, or group, that held them. Theodore "Dot" Babb, age 14, trained as a warrior and later surprised the Comanche when he went back to the white world. Another captive, Cynthia Ann Parker, married a chief and mothered the famous warrior chief Quanah Parker.

Cynthia Ann Parker

Parker's Comanche name was *Naduah*, meaning "keeps warm with us."

Conflict With Mexico

Up until the early 1800s, the Spanish government sought the Comanche as an **ally** against another raiding people, the Apache. The Spanish and the Comanche traded with one another as part of their agreement. Things changed in 1821, however, when Mexico gained its

Miguel Hidalgo y Costilla was a priest and the first leader of Mexico's uprising against Spanish control. He is called the father of Mexican independence.

independence from Spain. The Mexican government was unable to trade as much with the Comanche. The Mexicans also would not help them defend the Comancheria against other tribes. The Comanche people were furious.

By 1840, the Comanche and the Arapaho had made peace.

Members of the Comanche and the Arapaho tribes discuss the threat of settlers taking over their lands.

Determined to get revenge, the Comanche raided Mexican towns for horses and captives. The Mexican government answered by offering a **bounty** for every dead Comanche. In the north, other Plains peoples raided the Comancheria for horses. The Comanche were under pressure. They had to make peace with old enemies such as the Cheyenne and the Arapaho in order to fight the Mexicans to the south.

White Settlement

At the same time, American settlers began to arrive in Texas. Stephen F. Austin, the founder of modern Texas, formed the Texas Rangers to protect 700 settler families. But the Comanche continued to raid. White settlers still traded with the Comanche. But tensions rose as settlers in Texas refused to respect the borders of the Comancheria.

Comanche raiders once captured Austin, but released him. They took only his Spanish grammar book.

Stephen F. Austin

14

The Council House Fight

On March 19, 1840, 65 Comanches arrived at the **Council** House in San Antonio, Texas. The Texas government asked them to release Texan and Mexican captives. The Comanches gave them one—a 16-year-old girl who had been tortured during captivity. They said they had no control over captives held by other Comanche groups. The angry Texans jailed the Comanche leaders. In the fight that followed, around 35 Comanches died. The incident led to years of hatred and violence.

The fight that began in the Council House spread into much of San Antonio.

New gun models allowed white bison hunters to shoot the creatures from farther away.

At one time, there were 100 million bison on the Plains.

New Enemies

In the 1840s, the Comanche faced a new and terrible enemy: disease. By about 1850, **smallpox** and other illnesses had killed thousands of Comanches. On the Great Plains, meanwhile, white hunters slaughtered millions of bison for their skins. The U.S. Army supported the killing to rob the Plains people of a food source. By 1884, there were only about 325 wild bison left in the United States.

16

Surrender

The U.S. government
began to move the
Comanche onto land put
aside as reservations. To
get them to go, government
officials promised to stop
the bison slaughter. But when
the government broke its
promise, Comanche horsemen
attacked a group of bison

Quanah Parker was the son of Cynthia Ann Parker and a Comanche chief.

hunters in Texas. The U.S. Army rode out to stop the
Comanches and drive them onto the reservation.
They also imprisoned certain Comanche leaders to
prevent them from influencing their communities. In
1875, the last free Comanches, the Quahadi group
led by the warrior Quanah Parker, surrendered.

CHAPTER  **2**

How the Comanche Lived

The Comanche people lived in groups called bands, each containing several families. A small council of older men advised each band. These advisors were made up of men considered wise and experienced by the rest of the band. A council made important decisions such as where to hunt and when to make allies. In times of war, the band selected a chief to lead the warriors. As soon as the war ended, however, he ceased being chief.

← Older, respected Comanche men held special leadership roles in the family group.

19

Comanche Work

Comanche were hunters and warriors. A Comanche boy's childhood reflected the fact that the Comanche lived to fight. By the time a boy was five or six, he could ride a horse and was learning to use weapons. Most became warriors when they were teenagers. Comanche women worked hard. They cooked, skinned animals, raised children, set up camps, and transported household goods when it was time to move.

A young boy rides a wild horse in an attempt to break it.

20

In hard times, the Comanche hunted birds and ground squirrels.

The Comanche word for squirrel is *wokohwi* (pronounced WOH-koh-wee).

Food

In earlier days, Comanche women gathered plant foods such as roots, berries, acorns, and wild onions. The men, meanwhile, hunted. Once the Comanche became Plains horsemen, however, hunting and raiding became much more important. Hunters sought black bear, pronghorn, deer, and elk in addition to bison. Later, raiders stole longhorn cattle from Texas ranches. The Comanche also traded for maize (corn) and tobacco.

Comanche Cooking

Women prepared and cooked meat such as bison or deer. Meat was either roasted over a fire or boiled. To boil meat or vegetables, women dug a pit in the ground and lined it with the leathery stomach of a bison. The cook poured water into this cooking pot and placed heated stones inside until the water was hot enough to make stew. Later, the Spanish traded them iron kettles and copper pots that could be heated over a fire.

The Comanche and other Plains Indians dried extra meat by setting it out in the sun or by smoking it. This kept the meat from spoiling.

The poles of Comanche teepees were usually made of cedar or pine.

Teepees were waterproof shelters.

The Teepee

Most of the Comancheria was flat and dry. When possible, the Comanche lived near clear streams and rivers in shelters called teepees. Comanche women dug a fire pit inside the teepee during cold weather. Smoke escaped through a hole in the top. Because a group of women could put up or take down a teepee in minutes, it was the perfect structure for **nomadic** people such as the Comanche.

Making a Teepee Cover

A teepee is a tall shelter made from a frame of wooden poles and wrapped in a cover. Some native peoples preferred a cover made of thick bark from a birch tree. The Comanche used bison hides (skins) sewn together. Light and easy to keep warm or cool, the teepee was used by hunting peoples up and down the Great Plains. A large teepee might stand 15 feet (5 meters) high and stretch 30 feet (9 m) across.

1

2

3

Women started by spreading out the bison hide. Using a knife carved from antler or bone, they scraped away any fat and meat.

After the hide dried in the sun, the women would scrape off the hair and soak the hide in water. To soften it, they rubbed it with fat and animal brain.

The softened hide was cleaned in water before being smoked over a fire to dry. After that, the women sewed hides together to make the teepee cover.

Buckskins and Beads

A Comanche man walked in **moccasins** made of deerskin and bison hide. For clothes, he wore leggings and a **breechcloth**. The breechcloth had long pieces of buckskin that hung down from a leather belt and covered him in the front and back. Buckskin is softened animal hide. Buckskin often refers to clothes made from deer hide. However, skins from elk, moose, bison, and other animals can also be considered buckskin.

Comanche women were responsible for making clothing.

Some Comanche leggings featured fringe made from human hair or deerskin.

26

In cold weather, Comanche men wore heavy robes made from animal skins. They once went bare-chested in summer. This changed after they had contact with American settlers in the 1800s. Comanche men began to dress in buckskin shirts decorated with fringe or beads shaped into patterns. They began making breechcloths from cotton.

Comanche boys usually wore no clothing until around age nine, except in cold weather. From that age on, they dressed like the men.

One of the few times men would wear any type of headgear was in cold weather. Then they might wear fur caps, as this Plains man is.

Women's Clothes

Comanche women wore long-sleeved deerskin dresses fringed with buckskin and decorated with beads and pieces of metal. Their moccasins were like those worn by men. In winter, they added a layer of warm bison robes and put on bison-hide boots with fur linings. Young girls, unlike the boys, always wore a breechcloth. By the age of 12, they dressed like the women in their band.

Comanche women wore long dresses with wide sleeves.

Men groomed their hair with brushes made from porcupine tails.

Hairstyles

Comanche men paid a lot of attention to their hair. Men kept their hair longer than women and wore it in a pair of braids tied with colored cloth. Some even lengthened their own hair with horsehair or hair from their wives.

Braids were sometimes wrapped with fur.

Women, like men, parted their hair in the middle. Both men and women colored the part in their hair with paint or yellow, red, or white clay.

Jewelry and Other Decorations

Comanche men and women also decorated their bodies. Both pierced their ears and wore earrings made of silver or, in earlier times, slivers of shell. Other jewelry included necklaces and bracelets. The Comanche wore tattoos at times, but body paint was more popular. Often, a Comanche man painted himself with shapes and colors he had seen in dreams. On special occasions, women painted themselves around the eyes and lips, on the cheeks, and sometimes inside their ears.

This Comanche man is wearing a breastplate made from tube-shaped beads called hair pipes.

The Bison Headdress

Comanche men did not wear the feathered headdresses found in other Plains groups. In fact, they rarely wore anything on their heads at all unless it was very cold. One exception was a headdress made from a bison skull. To make one, the warrior removed all of the meat from the skull. The horns and part of the hair were left in place. A bison headdress was considered too special for everyday use. A Comanche man would wear one only in war.

Some buffalo-horn headdresses were decorated with feathers.

Dry moss sometimes served as diapers for Comanche babies.

Comanche infants were placed in carriers called cradleboards. Mothers could then carry their babies on their backs.

CHAPTER 3

Growing Up Comanche

The Comanche may have been the fiercest raiders on the Great Plains, but they showered love on their children, especially their sons. The Comanche were known for having well-behaved children and seldom punished them. Sometimes, though, it was necessary to keep them in line. Then, a parent might tell a tale of monsters who lived in caves and ate children who misbehaved.

Comanche children did not go to school. Instead, they learned by doing activities and watching older relatives.

The roles of men and women and boys and girls were clearly defined in Comanche culture.

Future Wives and Mothers

From a young age, girls followed their mother and mother's sisters, whom they also called mother. When playing with toys and dolls, the young Comanche girl pretended to do tasks such as making clothes and cooking meals. Around age 12, she learned to cook and sew. She also helped prepare bison skins and make teepees. The goal was to learn to be a wife and mother.

Grandfathers and Sons

Boys learned from their grandfathers because their fathers had to spend time away on hunts or raids. The Comanche considered horses so important that boys learned to ride by age five. Around that time, a boy also started to shoot a bow and arrow. He soon hunted birds and small animals with other boys in the band. His first bison hunt marked a major point on the path to adulthood.

The Comanche learned to load and shoot guns while on horseback.

Boys and young men were respected because they might one day lose their lives in battle.

Vision Quest

Around age 15, a Comanche boy left on a vision quest—one of the most important events of his life. For days he ate nothing as he walked in uninhabited mountains. A spirit would eventually appear to him. During this vision, the boy learned his life's path and received the **spiritual** power he needed for adulthood. When the vision was over, he returned to his band to take up adult duties.

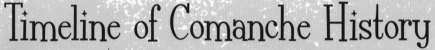

Timeline of Comanche History

1600s
Comanche split from Shoshone

1840
Council House fight

Becoming an Adult

A Comanche boy decided what skill to learn based on the vision's advice. This skill might be medicine or specialized fighting. Then he trained as an **apprentice** to an adult man. But it was through raiding and wars of revenge that he became a hero or warrior. It was then that his long childhood training paid off. His ability to take horses and captives, among other skills, earned him great respect.

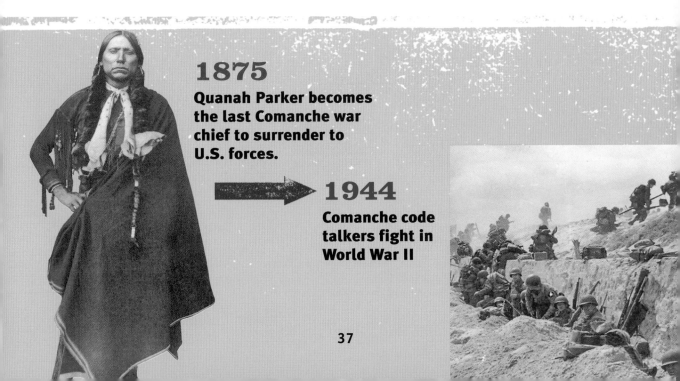

1875
Quanah Parker becomes the last Comanche war chief to surrender to U.S. forces.

1944
Comanche code talkers fight in World War II

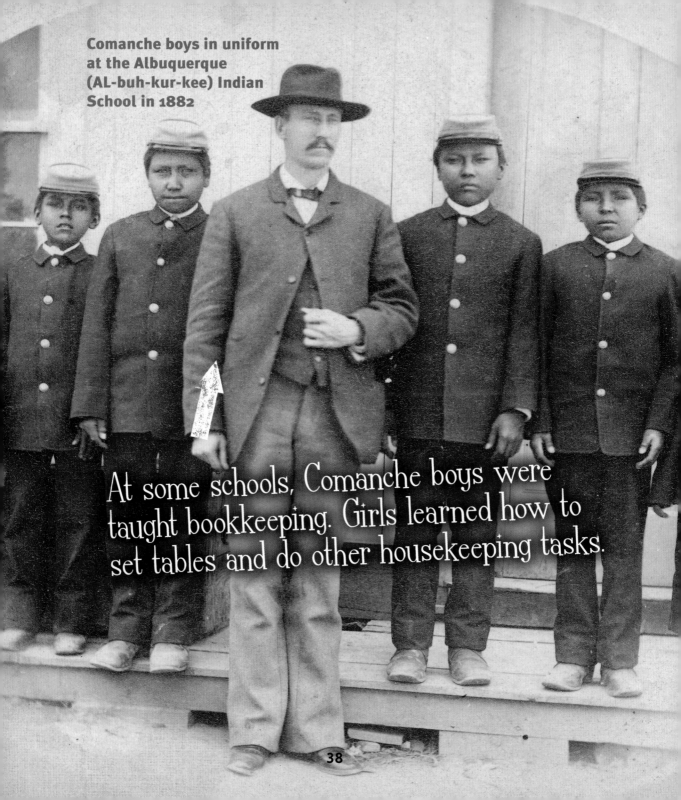

Comanche boys in uniform at the Albuquerque (AL-buh-kur-kee) Indian School in 1882

At some schools, Comanche boys were taught bookkeeping. Girls learned how to set tables and do other housekeeping tasks.

CHAPTER 4

The Comanche Today

Today, less than 1 percent of Comanches can still speak the Comanche language. Why? In the late 1800s, the U.S. government and churches put Comanche children in schools that were often far away from their homes. There, the teachers punished them for using any language except English. The children of those children grew up learning only a little of the Comanche language or none at all. Comanche, once spoken across the Great Plains, began to disappear.

Seventeen Comanche code talkers served in the U.S. Army during World War II.

In the 1930s, Germans attempted to learn certain Native American languages.

The Code Talkers

During World War I and World War II, the Comanche language became an important tool for the U.S. Army. Comanche soldiers created a secret code in their native language to keep important messages from falling into enemy hands. The Comanche language was so different from other languages that no one could crack the code. The work of these Comanche "code talkers" helped the United States and their allies to win both world wars.

Reservation Life

Today, about 14,500 members of the Comanche tribe live in the United States. About half of them live in the southwestern part of Oklahoma. The Comanche Nation is headquartered in Lawton, Oklahoma. The Comanche operate a number of businesses as well as a two-year college. They also have their own health and safety services.

LaDonna Harris (shown here in the 1970s) is a Comanche writer and activist. Throughout her career, she has worked to improve the lives of American Indians.

Preserving the Past

Today, Comanche work to make sure the culture of their people is preserved for the future. They keep records of the Comanche language so it will not be lost. They also operate museums and cultural centers where people can learn about Comanche customs and history. With their help, more and more people will be able to learn the story of the Comanche. ★

A young Comanche boy in powwow clothing. Powwows are gatherings that celebrate Native American culture.

Size of Comancheria in 1836: 240,000 sq. mi. (620,000 sq km)

Height of a large teepee: 15 ft. (5 m)

Average number of bison hides used in a teepee cover: 14

Population of Comanche in 1850: Between 7,000 and 12,000

Population of bison in 1500: About 30 million

Population of bison in 1884: About 325

Age a Comanche girl dressed like an adult: 12

Age a Comanche boy went on a vision quest: Around 15

Number of Comanche code talkers: 17

Number of Comanche words in army code: 100

Did you find the truth?

T Comanches played a vital role in World War II.

F The outer covering of Comanche teepees was made of heavyweight cotton.

Resources

Books

Birchfield, D. L. *Comanche*. Milwaukee: Gareth Stevens, 2004.

De Capua, Sarah. *The Comanche*. New York: Marshall Cavendish Benchmark, 2007.

Ditchfield, Christin. *The Comanche*. New York: Children's Press, 2005.

Egan, Tracie. *Cynthia Ann Parker: Comanche Captive*. New York: Rosen, 2004.

Englar, Mary. *Comanche Warriors*. Mankato, MN: Capstone, 2008.

George, Charles. *The Comanche*. San Diego, CA: KidHaven, 2003.

Rollings, Willard H. *The Comanche*. Philadelphia: Chelsea House, 2005.

Zemlicka, Shannon. *Quanah Parker*. Minneapolis: Lerner, 2004.

Organizations and Web Sites

The Comanche Nation of Oklahoma

www.comanchenation.com

Learn about Comanche history and find out what's going on today on the Comanche Reservation in Lawton, Oklahoma.

National Geographic: American Bison

http://animals.nationalgeographic.com/animals/mammals/american-bison.html

Find out more about the creature that was a source of many important products for the Comanche.

National Museum of the American Indian

www.nmai.si.edu

See exhibits about the lives and culture of Native Americans.

Places to Visit

Big Bend National Park— The Comanche Trail

PO Box 129
Big Bend National Park, TX 79834
(432)477-2251
www.nps.gov/bibe/history culture/comanche_trail.htm
Explore land that the Comanche once traveled when going on raids.

Comanche National Museum and Cultural Center

701 NW Ferris Avenue
Lawton, OK 73507
(580) 353-0404
www.comanchemuseum.com
Learn about Comanche history and culture through exhibits, arts, and videos.

Important Words

ally (AL-eye)—a country or person joined with another for a special purpose

apprentice (uh-PREN-tiss)—someone who learns a job from a skilled worker

bounty (BOUN-tee)—a reward given for capturing or killing someone

breechcloth (BREECH-kloth)—a piece of clothing that hangs down below the waist in the front and back

council (KOUN-suhl)—a group of leaders

independence (in-duh-PEN-duhnss)—a state of not being controlled by others

mobile (MOH-buhl or MOH-beel or MOH-bile)—able to move quickly and easily

moccasins (MOK-uh-suhnz)—soft shoes or boots with no heel

nomadic (noh-MAD-ihk)—having to do with people who move from place to place

reservations (rez-ur-VAY-shuhnz)—land set aside for use by Native Americans

smallpox (SMAWL-poks)—a deadly disease that causes aches, a fever, and red bumps to break out on the skin

spiritual (SPIHR-uh-choo-uhl)—having to do with religion

tradition (truh-DISH-uhn)—a custom or belief handed down from generation to generation

Index

Page numbers in **bold** indicate illustrations

About the Authors

Kevin Cunningham has written more than 40 books on disasters, the history of disease, Native Americans, and other topics. Cunningham lives near Chicago with his wife and young daughter.

Peter Benoit is educated as a mathematician but has many other interests. He has taught and tutored high school and college students for many years, mostly in math and science. He also runs summer workshops for writers and students of literature. Benoit has written more than 2,000 poems. His life has been one committed to learning. He lives in Greenwich, New York.